A Visual Dictionary of a
PIONEER
COMMUNITY

Bobbie Kalman

Crabtree Publishing Company
www.crabtreebooks.com

Crabtree Visual Dictionaries
Created by Bobbie Kalman

For Aunt Ditti, our family matriarch, on her 88th birthday
You are loved and respected by us all. I am especially grateful to have you in my life.

Author and Editor-in-Chief
Bobbie Kalman

Editor
Robin Johnson

Illustration research
Crystal Sikkens

Design
Bobbie Kalman
Katherine Kantor

Production coordinator
Katherine Kantor

Illustrations
All illustrations by Barbara Bedell except:
Valérie Appriousal: page 30 (flatboat and teamboat)
Halina Below-Spada: page 15
Antoinette "Cookie" Bortolon: back cover (milk can and iron), pages 1 (mortar and pestle), 3 (milk can, iron, plow, and cup and ball game), 9 (iron toaster, milk can, mortar and pestle, sugar cutter, and sugar cone), 13 (plow), 17 (top), 22 (carding paddles), 29 (mobcap, girl wearing pinafore, and boy), 30 (dugout canoe)
Jeanette McNaughton-Julich: page 30 (canal boat, keelboat, and hunters)
Trevor Morgan: back cover (cart), pages 9 (fireplace and pie safe), 18 (abacus)
Bonna Rouse: front cover (man and girl), pages 4 (top left and bottom right), 5 (all except village and horseshoe), 6, 7 (all except bottom right), 18 (slate), 19 (top right), 21 (top left and top middle), 23 (girl sewing sampler), 26 (drawknife and building), 27 (carpenter, tools, plane, and parts of wheel), 28 (top left and bottom right), 31 (top right)
Margaret Amy Salter: page 19 (flowers and rabbit)

Photographs and reproductions
© Currier & Ives: page 27
© Morgan Weistling/The Greenwich Workshop, Inc.: page 25
© Bobbie Kalman: page 26
© Shutterstock.com: pages 6, 7, 14, 23
Other images by Image Club Graphics

Library and Archives Canada Cataloguing in Publication

Kalman, Bobbie, 1947-
    A visual dictionary of a pioneer community / Bobbie Kalman.

(Crabtree visual dictionaries)
Includes index.
ISBN 978-0-7787-3504-5 (bound).--ISBN 978-0-7787-3524-3 (pbk.)

    1. Frontier and pioneer life--United States--Dictionaries, Juvenile.
2. United States--Social life and customs--Dictionaries, Juvenile.
3. Frontier and pioneer life--United States--Pictorial works--Juvenile literature. 4. United States--Social life and customs--Pictorial works--Juvenile literature. 5. Picture dictionaries--Juvenile literature. I. Title. II. Series.

E179.5.K35 2007   j973   C2007-906558-9

Library of Congress Cataloging-in-Publication Data

Kalman, Bobbie.
    A visual dictionary of a pioneer community / Bobbie Kalman.
        p. cm. -- (Crabtree visual dictionaries)
    Includes index.
    ISBN-13: 978-0-7787-3504-5 (rlb)
    ISBN-10: 0-7787-3504-4 (rlb)
    ISBN-13: 978-0-7787-3524-3 (pb)
    ISBN-10: 0-7787-3524-9 (pb)
    1. Frontier and pioneer life--United States--Dictionaries, Juvenile. 2. Community life--United States--History--19th century--Dictionaries, Juvenile. 3. Dwellings--United States--History--19th century--Dictionaries, Juvenile. 4. Material culture--United States--History--19th century--Dictionaries, Juvenile. 5. United States--Social life and customs--1783-1865--Dictionaries, Juvenile. 6. Frontier and pioneer life--United States--Pictorial works--Juvenile literature. 7. Community life--United States--History--19th century--Pictorial works--Juvenile literature. 8. Dwellings--United States--History--19th century--Pictorial works--Juvenile literature. 9. Material culture--United States--History--19th century--Pictorial works--Juvenile literature. 10. Picture dictionaries--Juvenile literature. I. Title. II. Series.

    E179.5.K365 2007
    973.03--dc22
                                    2007044309

Crabtree Publishing Company
www.crabtreebooks.com   1-800-387-7650

Published in Canada
Crabtree Publishing
616 Welland Ave.
St. Catharines, Ontario
L2M 5V6

Published in the United States
Crabtree Publishing
PMB16A
350 Fifth Ave., Suite 3308
New York, NY 10118

Published in the United Kingdom
Crabtree Publishing
White Cross Mills
High Town, Lancaster
LA1 4XS

Published in Australia
Crabtree Publishing
386 Mt. Alexander Rd.
Ascot Vale (Melbourne)
VIC 3032

Contents

A pioneer village

The first settlers had to cut down trees and move big rocks to make room for homes and fields.

A **pioneer** or **settler** is a person who moves into a new country or area to explore it or to **settle** there. To settle is to make a home and live in a place where few others live. The first settlers who came to North America had to cut down trees and build homes in the **wilderness**. They had very few tools and just a few animals to help them with their work. The settlers also had to grow their own food because there were no grocery stores. As more settlers moved into an area, **villages** grew. A village is a small **community**. Some people lived in the villages and opened shops there. Others visited the villages to trade extra foods they grew for things in the shops.

Gristmills were very important to the settlers. Grain was ground into flour at these mills.

Children attended schools in the villages.

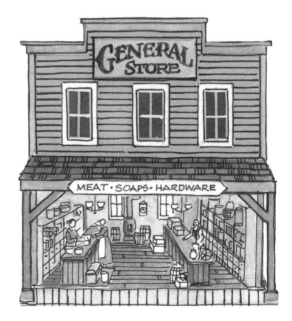

General stores carried many kinds of goods, such as food, clothes, and tools.

1. Many pioneers were farmers. They grew food and raised animals. They kept the animals in barns.

2. Pioneers used wagons for travel and for carrying goods. Broken wagons were fixed at wagon-repair shops.

3. When people traveled, they often spent the night at **inns**. An inn is like a hotel.

4. **Coopers**, or barrelmakers, made wooden barrels. People stored foods and drinks in the barrels.

5. **Blacksmiths** made things from a black metal called iron. They also **shod** horses, or put new shoes on them.

6. **Carpenters** made simple furniture such as chairs, tables, and dressers. They also made coffins and worked as **undertakers**.

barrel

horseshoe

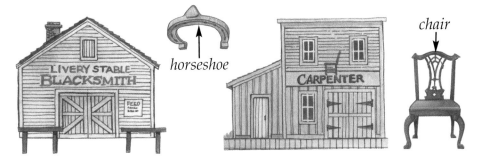

chair

5

Pioneer homes

log house

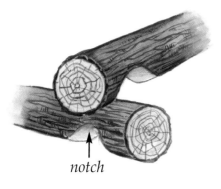

round logs

Some pioneers used trees to build log houses. They stacked up heavy logs to make the walls. This log cabin was made using round logs.

notch

*Pioneers made **notches** in the ends of the logs to keep them from moving or rolling off their houses.*

Pioneers who lived near forests made their first homes from the trees they cut down. They built their homes from logs, tree branches, straw, and mud. Once a community built a **sawmill**, the settlers could get logs cut into **planks**, or boards. Using planks, people could build houses that had two **stories**, or levels, and more than one room. Some settlers did not live near forests, however. In the West, the land was flat, with very few trees. The pioneers who settled this land had to make their first homes from **sod**, or grass and dirt. Sod homes had to be cut from the earth and were hard to build.

stone chimney

squared logs

straw

*This cabin was made with **squared logs**. The round parts of the logs were cut off with an ax. The chimney was made of stones.*

ax

The pioneers filled the spaces between the logs to keep out the wind and rain. They used straw, mud, grass, or wood chips to fill the spaces.

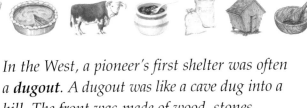

dugout

In the West, a pioneer's first shelter was often a **dugout**. A dugout was like a cave dug into a hill. The front was made of wood, stones, or sod. When it rained, the grassy roof of the dugout often became soggy. If an animal walked on the roof, it could fall into the house!

soddy

sod bricks

Pioneers in the West layered bricks of sod to make the walls of their homes. The sod was held together with mud. A home made of sod was called a **soddy**.

planks cut at a sawmill

frame house

People who lived near sawmills built **frame houses**. Frame houses were built by nailing planks to a wooden frame. This frame house has two stories and many rooms.

7

The kitchen

The kitchen was the "heart" of the pioneer home. In many homes, it was the only room. People ate in the kitchen and slept there, too. Even in larger homes, the kitchen was the center of family activity. Many jobs, such as **spinning**, **weaving**, and making candles, were done in the kitchen. People also read books, sang songs, told stories, and played games in this room. The kitchen fire was always burning. It made the room comfortable and cozy.

dried herbs

dishes

bread oven

butter churn

soup kettle

oil lamp

milk

potatoes

roasted chicken

corn on the cob

bread oven   andirons   crane

Breads and cakes were baked in a **bread oven**. **Andirons** held the logs in the fireplace. A **crane** held pots over the fire.

coffee grinder

Coffee beans were crushed in a **coffee grinder**.

spider

A frying pan with legs and a long handle was called a **spider**.

Bread was toasted in front of the fire using an iron toaster.

pie safe

Baked goods were kept in a **pie safe**. The pie safe protected the food from bugs and mice.

iron toaster

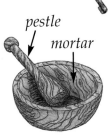

pestle   mortar

Spices were crushed using a **mortar** and **pestle**.

Making butter

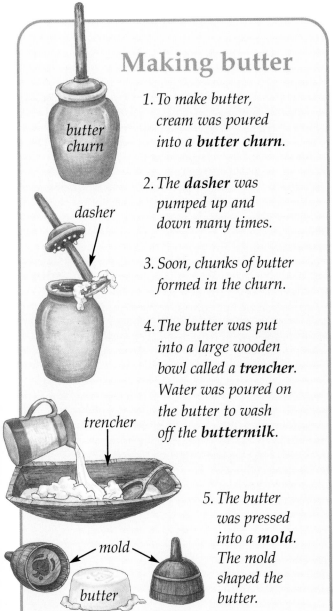

butter churn

dasher

trencher

mold   butter

1. To make butter, cream was poured into a **butter churn**.

2. The **dasher** was pumped up and down many times.

3. Soon, chunks of butter formed in the churn.

4. The butter was put into a large wooden bowl called a **trencher**. Water was poured on the butter to wash off the **buttermilk**.

5. The butter was pressed into a **mold**. The mold shaped the butter.

waffle iron

Waffles were baked over the fire in **waffle irons**.

Milk was poured into big metal jugs.

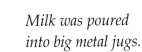

milk jug   sugar cone

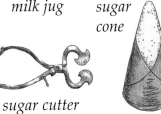

sugar cutter

Sugar was sold in cones. It was cut with a **sugar cutter**.

gunny sacks

Flour was kept in cloth bags called **gunny sacks**.

The pioneer farm

plank farm house

orchard

log house

barns

Most pioneers planted gardens behind their homes. They raised a few chickens and one or two cows. Some farmers, however, had big fields and several barns with different kinds of animals. The biggest barn on the farm was the center of activity. In this building, cows were milked, tools were repaired, and sheep were **sheared**. To shear sheep is to cut off their thick winter wool.

*Bundles of hay or straw were dropped down to the threshing floor through an opening called the **hay bay**.*

*Farmers stored hay and straw in the **hayloft**.*

sheep

pig

Equipment that was not being used was kept in the storage area.

cows

*The **threshing floor** was used as a work space.*

Grain was stored in wooden bins.

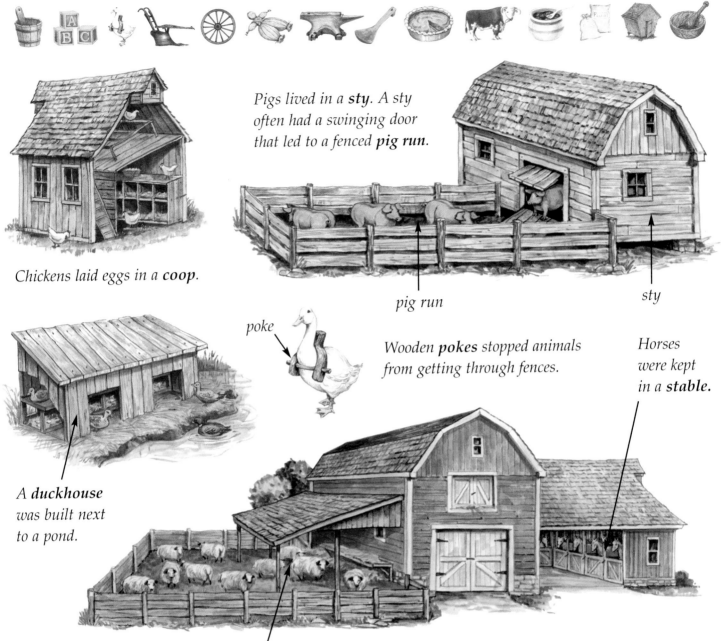

Chickens laid eggs in a **coop**.

Pigs lived in a **sty**. A sty often had a swinging door that led to a fenced **pig run**.

pig run

sty

poke

A **duckhouse** was built next to a pond.

Wooden **pokes** stopped animals from getting through fences.

Horses were kept in a **stable.**

A **sheep shed** protected sheep from the sun and rain.

A **springhouse** was built over a cold-water spring. Milk and other foods were kept in the water so they would not spoil.

A **corncrib** helped keep corn from going moldy. Air entered the building through holes in the walls and kept the corn dry.

A **smokehouse** was used to flavor meat and keep it from going bad.

Farm work and tools

Running a farm was hard work. The whole family helped. Children had lists of **chores**, or jobs, that they had to do every day. Chores included feeding animals, milking cows, collecting eggs, cleaning out barns, and helping in the gardens. Children learned which plants grew well together. They helped plant and gather the **crops**. They also peeled apples and **shucked** corn. To shuck is to remove the **husks**, or outer coverings, from the corn. Some of the tools that the farmers and their children used are shown on these pages.

*Weather vanes showed in which direction the wind was blowing. They helped farmers **predict**, or guess, the coming weather.*

Farmers used wooden rakes to gather straw and spread it across the barn floor for their animals.

Candles were placed in tin lanterns to prevent fires.

apple orchard

scarecrow

corn

pumpkins

planting seeds

gathering vegetables

12

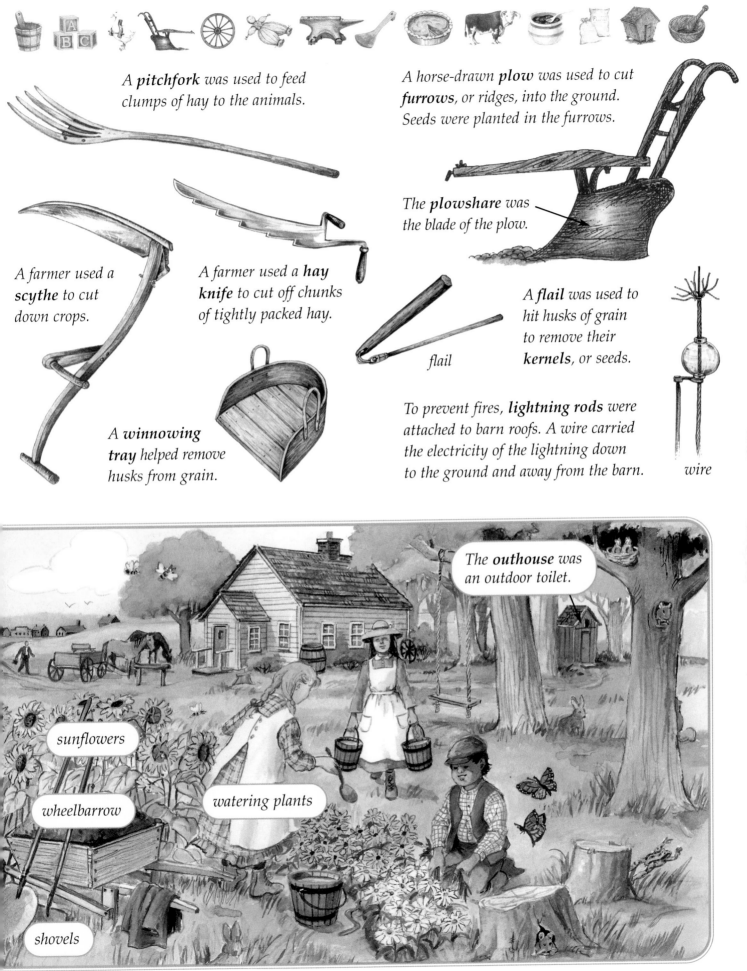

A **pitchfork** was used to feed clumps of hay to the animals.

A horse-drawn **plow** was used to cut **furrows**, or ridges, into the ground. Seeds were planted in the furrows.

The **plowshare** was the blade of the plow.

A farmer used a **scythe** to cut down crops.

A farmer used a **hay knife** to cut off chunks of tightly packed hay.

A **flail** was used to hit husks of grain to remove their **kernels**, or seeds.

flail

A **winnowing tray** helped remove husks from grain.

To prevent fires, **lightning rods** were attached to barn roofs. A wire carried the electricity of the lightning down to the ground and away from the barn.

wire

The **outhouse** was an outdoor toilet.

sunflowers

wheelbarrow

watering plants

shovels

13

The gristmill

Most settlers ate bread every day. Bread is made mainly of flour. Flour comes from grains such as wheat, corn, and rye. Before there was a gristmill in a community, pioneers had to **pound**, or crush, grain by hand. Grain is very hard, and it takes a lot of work to pound it into flour. A gristmill used the power of wind or water to crush grain into flour. People could take their grain to the gristmill and bring back sacks of flour for baking bread and cakes.

Corn was ground into flour at the gristmill.

Most people eat bread every day, just as the pioneers did.

Gristmills had three floors.

waterwheel

Different types of **waterwheels** were used in gristmills. A waterwheel was a huge wheel that had paddles or buckets on it. The most common type of waterwheel was the **overshot wheel**. This wheel was turned by water that **shot**, or flowed quickly, over it.

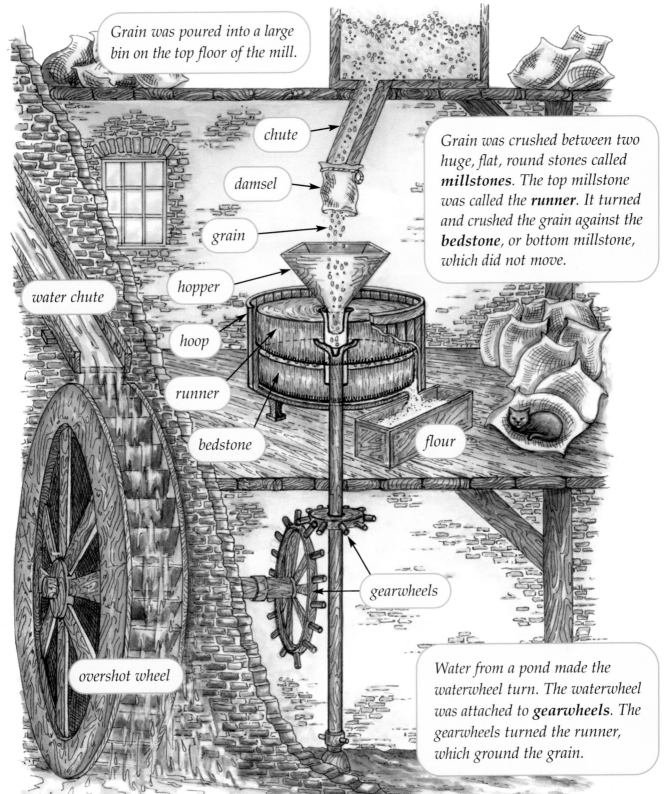

Grain was poured into a large bin on the top floor of the mill.

chute

damsel

grain

water chute

hopper

hoop

runner

bedstone

flour

gearwheels

overshot wheel

Grain was crushed between two huge, flat, round stones called **millstones**. The top millstone was called the **runner**. It turned and crushed the grain against the **bedstone**, or bottom millstone, which did not move.

Water from a pond made the waterwheel turn. The waterwheel was attached to **gearwheels**. The gearwheels turned the runner, which ground the grain.

15

THE GENERAL STORE

watering can

straw hat

lantern

brooms

fabric

barrel

The general store made life easier in a pioneer community. It gave farmers a place to trade their crops for the things they needed. It also helped a pioneer village grow. When a general store opened, **craftspeople** such as carpenters and blacksmiths also came to the area to open shops. The general store was the center of village life. People met there to shop and to hear the latest news in the community.

butter churn

cabbage

bag of flour

corn

apples

pumpkin

squash

jug

potatoes

The general store was also the post office. People sent and picked up their mail there. Men often played checkers at the back of the store while their wives shopped. People did not use money to buy things at the general store. They **bartered** instead. To barter is to buy or sell without using money. The storekeeper kept track of how much everyone needed to pay. The customers paid with flour, eggs, bread, or with crafts they made.

Make a list of 20 things that are for sale at this general store. Then list five things people would not use today. How were these things used by the pioneers?

nails

kitchen utensils

comb

lantern

hairbrush

pipe

soup kettle

glasses

soap dish

pocket watch

cutlery

children's toys

man's top hat

mail

fabric

pitcher and wash basin

glove

apples

hat

Children loved to go to the general store because they could get candy treats there.

lamp

dishes

candy

coffee grinder

The one-room school

When the first settlers arrived, there were no schools. Children helped their parents build homes and plant gardens. When more people moved into a pioneer community, the settlers built a schoolhouse for the children. The schoolhouse had only one room and one teacher. In a **one-room school**, children of all ages learned together. The girls sat on one side of the room, and the boys sat on the other side. The younger children sat at the front of the class. In early pioneer schools, the children shared desks. A stove heated the classroom.

abacus

slate

Children used **abacuses** to learn how to add and subtract.

They wrote their work on small boards called **slates**.

dunce cap

*A child who did not behave had to sit in the corner wearing a **dunce cap**. Dunce means silly or stupid.*

At school, children studied reading, writing, and math. They also learned about plants and animals.

In later times, pioneer schools had single desks.

This math game was called Buzz. When the teacher said "buzz," the children had to say the correct number. Which numbers have been replaced by buzzing bees?

Children looked forward to recess, when they could play outdoors.

This girl is writing her math answer on the blackboard.

Children's games

Pioneer children loved to play games! They played at recess, on the way home from school, and when they had some free time from their chores. There were very few toys in those days, so children played with simple objects such as ropes, hoops, and balls. They also played tag, hide-and-seek, leapfrog, hopscotch, and clapping games. Which of the games shown on these pages do you play with your friends?

dodge ball

*Why do you think this game was called **sardines**?*

leapfrog

*Could you **dodge**, or avoid, this ball?*

egg-in-the-spoon

three-legged race

push-the-potato

On the last day of school, there was a picnic. Races and games made the day fun!

Clapping games were very popular with girls.

hopscotch

Baseball came from a game called **rounders**. Rounders was played with a stick, a rock, and three posts.

This game was called **sticky apple**. The person who was tagged had to keep a hand on the spot where he or she was touched, while trying to tag others.

These children are playing a word game that is teaching them how to spell.

Children played skipping games. They sang rhymes to keep the beat.

21

Home crafts

Pioneers had to make many of the items they needed. Men and boys carved useful objects for the home. Women and girls learned skills such as spinning, weaving, and sewing, so they could make clothing and blankets. The pioneers did not throw anything away. They reused old materials and made other things, such as **quilts** and **rag rugs**, from them.

1. Pioneer women made clothing from sheep's *fleece*, or wool. The thick winter fleece was sheared off the sheep in spring.

fleece

2. The wool was fluffed between two **carding paddles** that were covered with short nails. The paddles removed dirt from the wool.

carding paddles

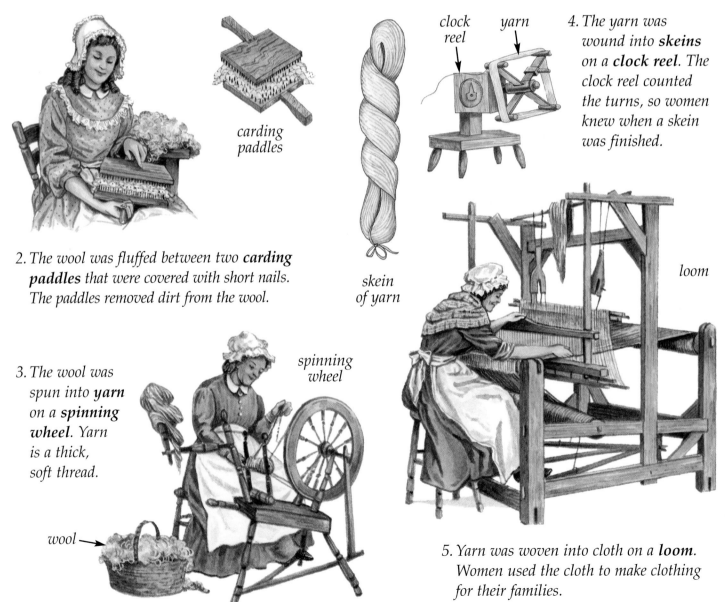

3. The wool was spun into **yarn** on a **spinning wheel**. Yarn is a thick, soft thread.

spinning wheel

wool

skein of yarn

clock reel   yarn

4. The yarn was wound into **skeins** on a **clock reel**. The clock reel counted the turns, so women knew when a skein was finished.

loom

5. Yarn was woven into cloth on a **loom**. Women used the cloth to make clothing for their families.

Rag rugs were made from **rags**, or old pieces of cloth. The rags were braided and then sewn together.

This rag rug is being woven on a loom. In the picture on the left, you can see how the woven rug looked up close.

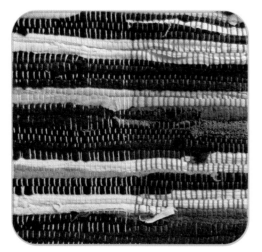

quilt

Old clothing was ripped into strips and used to make quilts. Quilts are blankets made from pieces of cloth. The pieces are sewn together to make a pattern.

Young girls practiced sewing on **samplers**. Samplers were pieces of cloth that had letters of the alphabet and Bible verses written on them.

sampler

Men and boys carved simple wooden furniture, such as stools for the home.

Work and play

apples

muffin

pumpkin pie

After working hard at bees, the pioneers enjoyed all kinds of tasty foods.

The pioneers made many things by hand. When there were big jobs to do, neighbors pitched in and helped one another. To make the work fun, pioneers held work parties called **bees**. There were building bees, corn-shucking bees, and quilting bees. After the work was finished, there was a huge meal and a lot of fun. Men challenged one another to contests of skill, women shared the latest village news, and children played games. Bees gave people a chance to see their neighbors, who often lived far away. The picture below shows a **barn-raising** bee, where neighbors worked together to build the frame of a barn.

roof tree   barn frame

*A small tree or branch was attached to the roof of the barn for good luck. It was called a **roof tree**.*

Women held quilting bees to make large quilts. After they finished a quilt, their families joined them for dinner.

Dancing was a part of many work parties.
This type of dance was called a **square dance**.

calling cards

Work parties were not the only time for visiting.
Young men visited young women on New Year's Day.
They left **calling cards** with their names on them.

25

The craftspeople

barrel

butter churn

bucket

Pioneers used barrels to store foods and drinks. They used buckets to carry liquids and butter churns to make butter.

In pioneer days, there were few machines. Almost everything was made by hand. The craftspeople in a pioneer community made items that were needed and used by the pioneers. Blacksmiths made things from hot iron. Coopers made buckets and barrels from wood. Carpenters made furniture and the wooden parts of houses. **Wheelwrights** made and repaired wagon wheels. **Harness makers** made saddles and **harnesses** for horses. Harnesses were straps that were used for riding horses or for attaching wagons to them.

*The cooper used a **drawknife** to shape wood and make it smooth.*

HARNESS MAKER

USED HARNESS

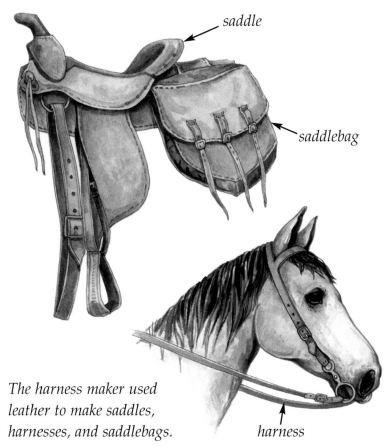

saddle

saddlebag

The harness maker used leather to make saddles, harnesses, and saddlebags.

harness

gouge

Carpenters used tools to make things from wood. This carpenter is using a **gouge** to make a pattern in wood.

A **plane** was used to smooth the rough parts of wood.

plane

a carpenter's tools

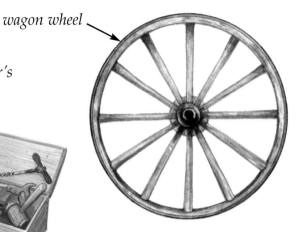

wagon wheel

Wheelwrights made wheels for wagons and carts. Pioneer roads were rough, so wheels broke often. Wheelwrights repaired broken wheels, as well.

hub   *felloe*

spokes

The blacksmith heated iron in a fireplace called a **forge**. He shaped objects on an **anvil**.

forge

wheel rims

anvil

The blacksmith gave old wheel rims to children. They used the rims in **hoop games**. The children chased rolling hoops and used sticks to keep the hoops from falling over.

Blacksmiths called **farriers** made horseshoes and nailed them onto the hoofs of horses.

ball peen hammer

horseshoe

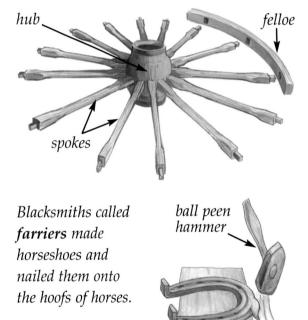

anvil

iron lantern

The blacksmith pounded iron on an anvil.

Pioneer clothing

Most of the clothing worn by the pioneers was made by hand. Summer clothes were made of cotton or **linen**. Linen came from a plant called flax. Winter clothes were made from sheep's wool. People who lived in the wilderness often wore **buckskin** clothing. Buckskin was made from deer **hides**, or skin. In pioneer villages, **yard goods** were sold at the general store. Yard goods were fabrics sold by the yard. Women sewed dresses, men's shirts, and coats from these materials. Most people had only two sets of clothes. One set was for work, and the other was worn to church.

Pants, shirts, and shoes were all made from buckskin.

smock

*Pioneer farmers wore loose shirts called **smocks**.*

cowboy hats

straw hat

overalls

suit coat

chaps

Ranch *workers wore jeans, cotton shirts, and cowboy hats.*

*Cowboys wore **chaps** to protect their legs and pants while riding through thorny bushes.*

*Many farmers wore **overalls** made of wool or linen.*

*Wealthy men wore suits made by **tailors**. Tailors sewed men's clothing.*

Pioneer women wore long dresses. At home, they always wore **aprons** to keep their dresses clean. Most pioneer women wore **bonnets** on their heads.

Soft linen caps (left) or **mobcaps** (below) were worn at home.

mobcap

poke

Outdoor sun bonnets were made of straw. This bonnet was called a **poke**.

bonnet

apron

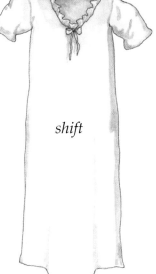

shift

drawers

Women's underpants were called **drawers**.

Women wore **shifts** under their clothes. They also slept in shifts.

Young girls wore big bonnets, short dresses, and **pinafores**. Pinafores were big aprons.

pinafore

collar

cuffs

blanket

Winter coats had fur collars and **cuffs**. This pioneer family is keeping warm under a blanket that is also made of fur.

On Sundays, boys wore suits that looked just like the suits their fathers wore.

Early travel

Travel in pioneer times was slow and difficult. There were few roads, and they were very muddy and bumpy. The first settlers built farms and villages along rivers and lakes. Traveling on water was much less difficult for the settlers than traveling over land. The settlers built a variety of boats to use on water. They also found ways to travel more easily on land.

*A **flatboat** carried passengers, their belongings, and their animals down shallow rivers.*

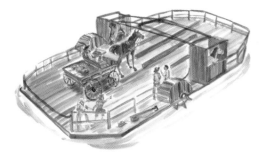

*A **teamboat** used horses that turned wheels as they walked. The wheels moved the boat forward.*

*The pioneers learned how to make canoes from the native peoples of North America. They carved **dugout canoes** from large tree trunks.*

*A **canal boat** was pulled by horses that walked on shore ahead of the boat.*

*A **keelboat** was a sailboat that was used on rivers.*

toboggan

snowshoes

*During the winter, pioneers wore **snowshoes** to walk on deep snow. Hunters carried animals on **toboggans**. Snowshoes and toboggans were first used by the native peoples.*

The settlers used **carts** and wagons to travel and to carry supplies. Simple carts were boxes with wheels attached. The carts were pulled by **oxen**.

oxen

cart

Corduroy roads and sidewalks were built so people would not sink into mud. They were made of logs and were very bumpy.

In winter, **stagecoach** wheels were replaced with **runners**. Runners were blades that could glide easily over snowy roads and frozen lakes.

stagecoach

sleigh bells

runner

covered wagon

wagon train

Pioneers who traveled to the West made the long trip in **covered wagons**. Many wagons traveled together. They formed long lines called **wagon trains**.

Glossary

Note: Many boldfaced words are defined where they appear in the book or are shown by pictures that are labeled.

blacksmith A person who makes things from iron by hand and repairs iron objects

buckskin The skin of a deer that has been softened to wear as clothing

buttermilk A sour, watery liquid that is left after butter has been churned

chaps Leather pants without seats worn by cowboys while riding horses

community A group of people who live in an area, as well as the area in which they live

corduroy road A bumpy road or street made of logs

craftsperson A person skilled in making certain things by hand

crop A plant grown for human use

ranch A large farm where horses, cows, or sheep are raised

sardines Small fish that are sold crowded together in cans

sawmill A place that saws logs into boards

settler A person who lives where there are very few other people; a pioneer

sod Soil with grass growing on it

spinning The act of turning fleece into yarn

undertaker A person who looks after dead people and arranges their funerals

weaving Making fabric from yarn on a loom

wilderness A natural area that people have not changed by building on it

Index